Windsor Smith
HOMEFRONT
DESIGN FOR MODERN LIVING

Foreword by Gwyneth Paltrow
TEXT BY MEREDITH STRANG

RIZZOLI
NEW YORK

New York · Paris · London · Milan

To my eternal love Anthony, for your incredible guidance and chivalry. I owe you most for always keeping the martinis chilled, for that first koi pond, and for making us all sit down to dinner as a family, no matter what. To my sons, Trinity and Oliver, with so much love for making every day since your birth extraordinary and inspiring; and for being my life gurus by refusing to accept any limitations. To my parents, Garry and Cathy Smith, for that first pair of tap shoes and for being proud that I was the odd sprout off the family tree.

CONTENTS

FOREWORD
By Gwyneth Paltrow

I fell in love with Windsor Smith before I ever laid eyes on her. It wasn't her grounded loveliness, or her sparkling personality; I would fall in love with the woman later. It was a house that did it.

I am a person who appreciates beautiful design and seeks it out, and I can get obsessive about it. One evening in London in the fall of 2012, I was at home, on the computer looking at houses (as I was wont to do) and I came across a house for sale in the Brentwood section of Los Angeles. Now, I am always looking at houses, more for pleasure than practicality, but when I saw this particular house, I felt something more than my usual covetousness. I felt the seas shift and the sky change.

On my next trip to Los Angeles, I went to see the house in person. It had been well documented in magazines, and I was excited to see it in the brick and mortar. The big garage gates swung open as the realtor buzzed me in, and there she sat, a one-story, white-brick beauty that took my breath away. As I walked through the front door onto a beautiful reclaimed stone floor from an old church somewhere in Peru, and absorbed the gentle shades of grey, I knew something deep and wonderful. I was home.

My love for the house continued to grow as I walked through each room. The house was magic, every detail well thought through: perfect proportions, flooded with light, antique floors and even a rotisserie in the kitchen. Not only could you see the thought and care and love for the house in its execution, you could feel it. My heart started to beat faster. Who was this Windsor Smith who had built a home so lovingly, and with such an incredible display of talent? When I finally met her, it all became clear.

I did indeed buy the house, and my love for it precipitated massive change in our lives. We left London for the sunnier climes of Los Angeles, but really, for the comfort and sanctity of the house that Windsor built.

After the closing, Windsor and I started to meet regularly to talk about furnishings. We would spend hours agonizing over swatches and profiles, delighting in the beauty of antiques and chairs. I pushed her into slightly more contemporary territory, and she expanded my appreciation for the traditional. During the many months of back and forth, Windsor's questions to me would often veer away from color palettes and curtains, and I came to know her essence through these queries. "How many nights a week do you cook?" she would ask. "Where do your kids to their homework?" I started to see that a beautiful home is only truly beautiful if it is serving the togetherness of the family, a concept that previously I had never paired with good design. I realized something very profound: Windsor's talent was not only artistic, it was intuitive. Her goal was to create a space for us to love in, not just live in. From that beautiful mindfulness, together we created a hybrid that worked perfectly, a house where family, and how we live, is the focus. A house where entertaining is natural. A house where, upon entering, you know you are home.

INTRODUCTION

There's a reason "Home, Sweet Home" has been such a common and instantly understood concept for ages; the metaphor of home is probably the most powerful in human existence. Home isn't only our territory, a physical place where we retreat to and spend our time, it also defines us as individuals and families—it truly is a "sense of place." Over the centuries we've given it its own guardians and gods, become "sick" when we've been away from it for too long, and held it as a welcoming hearth for our warriors to return to. With every child's growth mark on the frame of a closet door, it's become a tangible testament to the passage of time, and a keeper of the stories and rituals of the people who've lived there. Our homefronts show where we've been, and their support structure provides us with a springboard into life, defining who we will become.

Years ago I coined the phrase "lifestyle architect" because I needed a new way to express what I thought my role in the design world should be: to inspire people through repurposed rooms, to help them realize their dreams through design, and to show them ways to live in their homes that they never thought possible. Everyone has an individual and unique story, whether we

Hallways are often overlooked, but you can make the ordinary extraordinary with the addition of just one simple piece that tells a unique story. And do keep it simple: adding details for their own sake doesn't guarantee elegance and you'll miss what matters in the clutter. In a busier space you wouldn't see how the escutcheon on the settee leg connects with the design of the boiserie paneling.

are single, part of a couple, or have a growing family, and our homes should reflect that.

My goal is to design beautiful rooms for the way people today actually use them, regardless of their intended purpose, breaking the rules as to how a room "should" function. Technology has forever altered how we live, and many living plans have not kept pace with this development. We are left trying to design around spaces that used to work, or only ever worked for someone else, but no longer reflect our current needs. Today's families need deeply personalized, elegant spaces in a balanced, supportive environment in which they can grow and express themselves, but without having to sacrifice that vital connection to the present.

I didn't become a designer through a formal education or growing up in an exotic culture—I sort of snuck up on it, and my journey was purely intuitive. I grew up in Kansas and Texas, chock-full of dreams and completely oblivious to any shortcomings or limitations I might have had. I loved theater and dance; I eventually taught in Manhattan and Tokyo before moving to Los Angeles. While looking for architectural pieces and antiques in local flea markets to furnish my own home, I became acquainted with numerous dealers who were hosting what they called "Cheap and Chic" parties—think Tupperware or Naughty Lingerie events, but with vintage furniture and other objects.

One of them encouraged me to travel to France to expand my search area—so I flew to Paris, jumped in a rented truck, and headed south through the Pyrenees into Spain and then back again, literally pillaging the entire countryside. I realized I needed to offload some of my loot, and remembered that interior designer Kathryn Ireland, who I'd befriended at a "Mommy and Me" class in Los Angeles, had a country house in nearby Toulouse. Talk about serendipity—not only was she at home, but she let me store all of my treasures in her barn until they could be shipped by container to California.

For the next two years I traveled to Europe many times; I set up shop in West Hollywood as an antiques dealer, selling my finds from a warehouse, which is how I met my first clients and started buying for their homes. But I didn't just bring home twee knickknacks and the usual furniture, I returned with enormous architectural elements: headers, columns, big iron gates—and transformed them. A massive door frame became a huge pier mirror; discarded cornices and carved moldings were reincarnated with a new use of shape, color, and function. My somewhat impractical mantra was: "If it doesn't weigh over a thousand pounds, I won't buy it." And in the process I realized I'd not only found a gap between the conventionally static, overly formal gold-and-forest-green interior design of the time and what people were actually yearning for, but I'd also accidentally become an interior designer by working in the trenches.

On one of those long flights to Paris I was reading about Elsie de Wolfe in Tapert & Edkin's *The Power of Style*. Elsie was the first person to pave the way—before she came along, "designer" as an occupation didn't exist. In her day, décor was high Victorian: gloom, densely patterned wallpaper, heavy velvet draperies, gloom, dark wood paneling, lots of clutter, hideous bric-a-brac (the more, the better), and gloom. Elsie's clean-looking rooms—painted in fresh, light colors, with easy, relaxed furniture upholstered in pale tones and animal-print chintz—astonished society. She crossbred food, fashion, and the arts, introduced the concept of the cocktail party and the intimate dinner party, and did her easy entertaining in an environment characterized by those luxurious, refined furnishings, potted palms, and delicate gilded frames hung on pale chinoiserie-papered walls.

Even more importantly, she was the first person to use the word "lifestyle"—she quite literally changed the way people lived. I'm inspired by her passion for shattering taboos and getting rid of outdated notions of the way a house should be. I want to knock down conventions and open up rooms so they work with the way we live now. I don't aspire to create beautiful rooms for people, as much as I want to change the way we *live* in them.

When creating a homefront of your own, it's important to look beyond shimmery surfaces, gorgeous fabrics, and expensive furnishings, and think about the overall appeal of your home and what you want the quality of your life to be. It isn't just about pretty rooms anymore.

DESIGN
INTUITION

F rom the outset, what struck me the most was the extent to which many of my clients were expected to shoehorn their lifestyles into homes where somebody else (usually the builder or architect) had made all the decisions. Far too many were based on outdated models of how the "typical" family lived and entertained. The result was that my clients would find themselves in homes with insufficient closet space and a requisite dining room that might be lucky enough to see action for Thanksgiving and a few other special events, but would otherwise sit empty.

People need to be connected to their chosen lifestyle, rather than blindly adhering to a living plan that is fundamentally at odds with their actual way of life. Rather than squeezing square pegs into outdated round holes, rooms should be designed for how they are actually used, regardless of what their original "intended" purpose was. I recently did a home that had a lovely second-story room: it had amazing open woodwork details and great windows and light, and could have easily become a charming little attic-style space with toile-covered walls. While that would have looked very decorative, there wouldn't have been a lot of purpose to the space. I had an odd vision of it as a garden room, which is pretty much unheard of for an "upstairs" space, but I decided to roll with this "opposite" idea. The room's intent informed the color palette, so the beams were painted a spring garden green. Natural linens were used throughout, a vintage worktable went underneath the window, and gorgeous planters were stored below that. The whole room now had a theme and purpose, and my client, who was a garden enthusiast, now knew just how she could use this space and make it even more her own.

Nothing is sadder than a room that isn't working, or has otherwise become a dead zone. To get the most out of a space, it's vital to take advantage of its best features; every inch of our homes should be used to their fullest potential. Natural light is always a critical factor in design, so spend time watching where the sun rises and sets in your home and devise a floor plan that takes advantage of it.

In the past, people adhered to a more formal social routine, with rooms having a specific purpose or time of day in which they were used. The aptly named "morning room" was a casual reception and sitting room with an eastern exposure where the family would gather after breakfast and callers could be entertained. The allure of sunbeams filling a room early in the day is still timeless and irresistible, which is why the notion of the morning room is fashionable again now that more people are working from home.

If a room gets that beautiful morning light, turn it into a space that is conducive to early-in-the-day activities that suit you—be it a breakfast room, a spa, or a fitness studio for exercise or yoga. Your particular lifestyle should dictate how the space is used, even if the end results are unconventional or "outside the box."

A morning room is transitional; it's a launch point into your day, so set yourself up for success in every respect! The quality of morning light is very strong and direct, so when you choose a color, make it one that's easy on the eyes. Choose a favorite that you want to see first thing in the morning; pale orchids and blues, in particular, are wonderful colors to ease you into the day. Consider selecting fabrics that have a slight iridescence, like silvered linen, and have them backed so you can use them as wall coverings.

Slipcovers in cotton and linen that are barely a step away from bedding will make leaving yours a little more bearable—softness is the note to follow, so avoid tight, taut surfaces and edges.

The entry of my home is where you'll find some of my most valued personal treasures: a stunning, large Venetian beveled mirror I bought in Paris years ago, and an ornate silvered lantern suspended by a long chain. Both have claimed their rightful place in the entryways of my last four houses. Every time I arrive home, I'm welcomed by these favorite pieces, which just reinforces the most important advice I can give: Always decorate with objects you absolutely love.

A foyer is more than just a pass-through, it's the first impression people have of you and your home.

The old adage "you never get a second chance to make a first impression" is never truer than when it comes to entrances and powder rooms. I love a little formality in my entryway, hence the marble floors and classic round, tufted tête-à-tête settee that encourages visitors to linger and chat. (I freely admit that it's also a not-so-thinly-disguised homage to favorite resort hotels on the French Riviera!) Topiaries and outdoor obelisks bring the garden into the house. Our dog Zona loves the well-traveled space; she knows it's an ideal spot to get attention as friends and family come and go.

17

Diaphanous, swaying, seductive sheers at the windows will not only enhance the light, they will float and billow in the slightest breeze like gauzy sails, letting you see the wind's moving eddies and traceries. A large ceiling fan with propeller-like vanes that stir the air will transform your room into a lyrical, dancing space.

The concept of the drawing room as a family sitting room and reception area for afternoon callers (as well as a place the women had to "withdraw" to after a dinner party, leaving the luckier men to the brandy and cigars!) has fallen by the wayside, but trust me, the underlying principle is still sound. The side of the house where the sun sets is the ideal location for a family room that can double as a party setting—for everyone! The fading light is softer at the end of the day; four o'clock is known as "magic hour" in photography because the warm color of the low, almost-setting sun enhances everything. Shapes and textures can be more solid and substantial in counterpoint to the fading light; nothing looks quite as lovely as ornate brocade at sunset. Classic, sophisticated colors like darker blues, bronzes, and grays look amazingly different in the soft light of a lowered lamp or a candle; now is the time for mirrors and chandeliers to show what they can really do to illuminate a room and flatter its occupants.

When I first started out as a designer, it was in the heyday of the McMansion-type home, and many couples were requesting master suites with separate "his" and "hers" dressing areas and bathrooms. And why not? They certainly had the space. Fast forward a few years to a not-too-surprising phenomenon. Those same "separate everything" couples started calling me to design their separate houses—post-divorce. Meanwhile, most other clients who'd opted for shared bathrooms and dressing spaces were still together. I realized then what fashion and a floor plan can do to separate people, and what design can do to bring them together again.

(*opposite and following spread*) Relaxed yet sophisticated, this gracious Federal-inspired entry hall has a refined, old world feel, and was designed to be wide enough to serve as a dining room for as many as thirty guests. It's a creative solution for entertaining on a grand scale—for that handful of times a year when you actually throw a huge dinner party. While the average hallway doesn't usually see natural illumination, this one runs the length of the house, with French doors at the end welcoming light and air into the home. An oversized antiqued mirror expands the already generous proportions of the space; the Directoire-inspired glass transoms over the doorways carry the diamond floor motif into the adjacent rooms.

I don't aspire to create beautiful rooms for people, as much as I want to change the way they live in them.

Every project needs an inspiration, a story that you can create a design around. I wanted to design and build an elegant home that was also an equestrian property, so I imagined what the house would look like if a modern-day Slim Keith lived there with her family. While they led a busy and involved life, they had their horses in a dressage stable out back, along with everything they could ever desire in a country club. True luxury in design is when sport, lifestyle and beauty all come together seamlessly in the home.

Don't ignore the infinite
possibilities of the kitchen—
a place where we spend so
much time should be as elegant
as any other room in the house.

Designed to delight the dedicated chef, the industrial look of this high-functioning space is tempered with beautifully refined features like marble walls, countertops, and deep farm-house sinks; silvered sconces and vintage task lamps elevate the lighting to a thing of beauty. A mini-island doubles as a serving table, and three distinct stations reduce clutter and mess so that the kitchen runs like a well-oiled machine. The distressed surface of the rustic and reclaimed French oak planks impart a wonderful sense of history to the large and open area.

(*following spread*) Brass pendant lights with pleated black shades are just some of the warm notes that contrast with the cooler tones in the room. The pièce de résistance is the extra-long marble-topped refectory table. An upholstered wing chair presides over an eclectic group of leather-cushioned Savonarola-style seating and vintage metal café chairs; the irreverent juxtaposition results in a collected, fun feeling.

(*above and opposite*) One way to elevate a utilitarian space into everyday elegance is with beautiful hardware—it's the jewelry of the house. These gorgeous polished cabinet pulls with contrasting blackened nickel accents above the wet bar, which has a hammered metal prep sink and built-in espresso machine, delight the eye and prove that nothing is "too good for everyday" use. Gleaming metal surfaces are naturally associated with kitchens; backsplashes of antiqued mercury-glass mirrors not only satisfy that expectation but give the illusion of a more open, windowed space.

(*previous spread*) People who enjoy an equine life spend countless hours with their beloved animals, so their barns and paddocks are truly part of their living quarters. Paintings, drawings, and photographs adorn the walls behind comfortable old leather couches; competition ribbons, trophies, saddles, and blankets are stacked high over wooden feed bins and rustic tables. They are more than mere stables: they are art studios, libraries, and even sleepover lofts for slumber parties.

Nothing beats the allure of a stable. The rich textures in the hand-woven and quilted materials, the gleaming suppleness of the leathers, the myriad blanket colors, and the rhythm of the rows of stalls make them visually appealing. Their perfect juxtaposition of regimentation and casual disorder, polish and patina, matte and reflective, light and dark makes them welcoming, magical places.

I believe in the aperitif. The civilized hour of the cocktail is a time-honored tradition that lends itself to a perfect, personalized ceremony.

Whether it's a cart, cabinet, or a simple tray, the optimal bar setup is easy to achieve. My latest design twist utilizes gleaming silver-plated fireguards on a base—it's not only an extremely practical presentation, it evokes the elegance of deluxe railway car detailing and appeals to my love of layered elements. As for filling that space: classic decanters with stoppers of horn or silver that contain more essential liquors are an ideal accent for the many interesting and unusual bottles that house today's fun new concoctions.

(*following spread*) It's not about getting sloshed before, during, or after dinner à la *Mad Men*, but celebrating a ritual that's confined to a single drink (or mocktail!) with some style and enjoyable pageantry. So often we dismiss older rituals or traditions, without realizing the purpose they served. By deliberately calling a halt to rushing around, and taking the time for one perfect preprandial glass, you take the tempo down a little and allow some time to pause and reflect on the day.

THE ANNOTATED SHAKESPEARE

CLASSIC COUNTRY ESTATES

VILLA GARDENS of the MEDITERRANEAN

HOUSES

LUXURY HOTELS

VENETIAN PALAZZI

JEAN-MICHEL FRANK

Chests and secretaries in the foyer are a versatile way to hide clutter, but top them with a marble surface and you'll have a wonderfully finished look—as well as an impromptu bar or serving area.

Enlarge your entertainment footprint by making your entryway part of the experience. Take a tip from grand hotels like the Cap d'Antibes and greet visitors with verbena tea or something equally refreshing upon arrival—or just indulge in your own relaxation ritual, no vacation required! There's nothing more welcoming than greeting someone with, "What would you like to drink?" I like the idea that friends and guests are met at the door and pampered from the start.

(*following spread*) I love dark, dreamy bedrooms; like a naughty back booth in a dimly lit restaurant, their seductiveness positively encourages racy behavior! Don't be afraid of the dark—highly polished metallic and mirror finishes come alive against it, and there's no restriction on how they can be combined. A large mirror adds depth to a room by creating a portal or an additional doorway, and its reflection can literally double the pleasure of a great work of art. Groups hung symmetrically act as a focal point to ground a room; I instantly feel at home in a space that has mirrored walls facing one another.

The powder room may be small, but it can speak volumes in the way you offer guests your distinct brand of hospitality.

We rarely use our own powder rooms; outside of changing the towels and dusting the mirror, they're usually forgotten right after the last car has left the drive. Use the smaller space to experiment with a daring color or an expensive hand-painted wallpaper, and hang some of your most exquisite art on the walls to create a jewel box of a room. Pipe in some Serge Gainsbourg, provide flattering lighting as well as the most luxurious hand towels and Jo Malone soaps and hand lotions, and choose some fabulous fresh flowers. In short, make the room a mini-sanctuary—an oasis rather than a lonely desert outpost.

(*previous spread*) A bygone era undergoes a modern update in this elegant country home in New York's historic Tuxedo Park. The white walls and black-stained original flooring in the large center hall create a connecting gallery setting, allowing the owner's ever-changing collection of artwork to float in and out of the easy space. A spare and open minimalism lets the ever-present subtle notes of history shine: the scroll-back dining chairs with their streamlined animal legs are a modern interpretation of the Napoleonic Egyptian Revival style.

Reminiscent of a private train car on the Orient Express or a first-class suite on the *S.S. Normandie*, the updated master bath in this historic Gilded Age home is all about luxury accommodation. Clever mirror placement encourages an exclusive gentlemen's-club vibe while making the space seem far more generous than it actually is. Blackened steel and sterling silver finishes add a note of classic elegance to the no-nonsense masculine accouterments; that admirable restraint is challenged by the nautical-map-pattern of sweeping waves and intricate veining in the exuberant and eye-catching marble.

People shouldn't have to blindly adhere to a living plan that is fundamentally at odds with their actual lifestyle.

The formal dining room isn't missed in this home: everyone in the family plays an instrument, so a drum set, a piano, and guitars cozy up to the extra wide and deep lounge chairs and sofa in perfect harmony. The ebony-and-ivory keys inspired the color scheme of crisp white ottoman and black pony-skin seating; that palette is repeated in the grand-scale stylized graffiti canvas by Retna that floats atop the soft gray and white plaster damask wall.

48

Layering different textures, finishes, patterns, and styles achieves an elegant and comfortable aesthetic.

(*previous spread*) If there was no such thing as a male boudoir before, there is now—and it's the last word in masculine elegance. The air of ancestral smoking jackets and après-hunt leisure still lingers in this gentleman's dressing room, where the Jazz Age meets its jet-setter descendants—with the approval of all concerned. The afternoon sun softly caresses the tufted-leather waterfall sofa and highlights the fretwork pattern in the silk rug; metal accents so polished that they feel like art pieces reflect the warm glowing wood of the mid-century wardrobe.

A weathered bench with plenty of personality celebrates the marriage of rustic texture and modern color in this stone-floored mudroom. Equestrian accents of boots, harness, and helmets show to advantage against the glossy walls in classic navy blue; textured bins and baskets easily contain everyone's accessories and must-haves for outdoors. The repurposed brass train luggage rack with its versatile hooks becomes the perfect perch to receive that tossed riding crop or discarded velvet hard hat.

(*above and opposite*) This rustic side entry space grew up to be more than just a laundry room. The countertops afford plenty of room for vintage vases and jugs; the durable reclaimed stone floor and a view of the
greenery outside create an inspiring garden alcove. The pleated, plaid-taffeta-skirted deep flower sink
and fanciful upside-down flowerpot light fixtures bring a note of whimsy to an otherwise utilitarian space.

(*following spread, left and right*) Fragrant with lavender, the nature preserve that surrounds this
Hamptons retreat makes this outdoor living room a delight for the senses. Vibrant, on-trend
"exterior" fabrics allow the home's footprint to be enlarged beyond its four walls;
unconventional "indoor" colors work their magic by encouraging that domain to stretch far, far away.

(*above, opposite, and following spread*) It's important to engage all the space in a room, not just the horizontal aspects. By hanging the hull of a vintage crew boat from the ceiling in the living room of this Southampton home, the eye is drawn upward to such a fantastic—and setting-appropriate—outdoor sporting element. Bespoke architectural high-rise bookcases of gilded metal and gray-green leather, an enormous French 1940s églomisé mirror above the fireplace, and even the vertical elements in the artwork over the chest of drawers ensure that the commanding proportions of the room truly soar. A palette inspired by natural elements right outside its doors—bleached sand, weathered driftwood grays, the evening sky, and the soft blues of the water—brings the surrounding beach and ocean into the house and creates a comfortable, soothing, and infinitely approachable venue.

(*opposite and above*) The 1930s urn and pedestal in the hallway are crafted from shells, and the nine-teenth-century French daybed adds to the nautical theme of the home. The collection of unusual animals and birds, including this series of whimsical cast-iron monkeys cavorting between the exposed dishes, evolved gradually and organically; they all strike a unique note and add to the easy and elegant atmosphere. Open shelving encourages less clutter in the kitchen, as well as allowing the display of much-loved and used items. The result is an intensely personal yet easy, open, and approachable space.

ALL-EMBRACING SPACES

One of the things I hear most from families is that they want to spend more time together, so I try to design rooms that can embrace everyone—mom, dad, kids, and teens. It's vital to incorporate areas in a house for everyone's leisure pursuits, whether it's a pottery studio, a music room, a cozy reading corner, or a well-equipped kitchen for creating gourmet meals.

Face it: technology has had a hypnotic influence on us ever since the 1950s, when people first abandoned the family dinner table to eat their evening meals on trays in front of the TV. Technology still drives most of what we do, and we're connected more than ever. Thanks to 4G, Wi-Fi, and new lightweight mobile gadgets being born every five minutes, "anywhere" and "everywhere" is the new office. Personal environments are now doubling as workspaces, so people have abandoned the formal computer desk in the study to sit with their numerous devices at the kitchen table, lounge with them in front of the TV—or even to retreat with them to the bedroom. And as any parent who has a texting teenager at the dinner table will tell you, the same technology that promised to break down barriers and bring us together is now, ironically, pushing us farther apart.

The way to encourage and reestablish face-to-face time is by repurposing spaces, and rooms that multitask are often the perfect solution. By creating morning rooms, libraries, game rooms, and open-plan, layered spaces in the kitchen and other areas that inspire creativity and togetherness, these newly defined, all-embracing spaces serve as a hub for family activity.

Since the old-fashioned conventional dining room is a frequent culprit, the first step to fixing this problem is to unbutton it and get more use out of an overly formal space. Consider enlarging the kitchen to absorb it and make it more of a gathering place. I first realized that the two spaces could—and frequently should—become one, when I had a client who was downsizing. Since her furniture was too large for the new space, we knocked out a wall, brought in a long antique farm table, and hung her favorite chandeliers above it. The final look was a fun and provocative mix of rustic and cosmopolitan.

The growing popularity of open kitchens demonstrates that they shouldn't be hidden away anymore—day or night, kitchens are always where the action is. I work at home, and it's where we eat breakfast and lunch, take meetings and coffee breaks, and open our laptops and work. Then as the sun begins to set, we dim the lights and have friends over for cocktails and dinner—all in the same space. When you're entertaining it seems like everyone always ends up in the kitchen anyway, so don't stint when it comes to comfort or décor—use a sophisticated palette like gray or navy, and stock it with special refinements like hotel silver, china, and crystal goblets. After all, any room in which we spend so much time should be just as beautiful and elegant as any other space in the house!

If the dining room isn't in close proximity, look at the spaces adjacent to the kitchen, such as the doorways, to see if they can be widened, or if there's a wall that can be knocked down or a maid's room or butler's pantry that can be sacrificed to make the kitchen larger. Then bring in the biggest table you can, because that's really the lodestar that everything revolves

This living room was such a diaphanous whisper of a space that it called out for some serious grounding, and this provocative wingback chair doesn't disappoint. Covered in deep pewter silk-velvet that packs a lovely wallop of contrasting earthy color, it's a unifying element that still manages to stand on its own. The unusually shaped back complements the shape of the raised piano lid in the center of the room.

(*following spread*) Despite its light-filled and lovely lines, the room had previously failed to attract family activity, but once the piano was liberated from its corner pocket to take proud center stage, it provided a focal point for the room and opened up its myriad possibilities. The softly cascading sheers at the windows give the light a tactile quality while their height emphasizes the floating, weightless feel of the space.

around. Long refectory-style tables work like a magnet to bring people together—"refectory" refers to a group dining area, but the original Latin term means "a place one goes to be restored." The name says it all: these large central tables are where you have the meaningful meals, where the kids can spread out all of their homework, and where family problems are solved.

So what can you do with that dusty, unused dining room if it's not in proximity to the kitchen? You could dismantle it and turn it into a family room or library, but maintaining some flexibility in those spaces is crucial so that you won't have to make reservations when it comes time to entertain. On those handful of times a year when you're entertaining a bigger crowd, make sure your library or even the entry hall is wide enough to accommodate a party. Put a banquet table in the center, dim the sconces and the chandelier, and you've got a unique and dramatic space for entertaining.

Be aware of "cold spots"—spaces that aren't used as much as they could be due to lighting, furniture placement, or designation—and be open-minded about solutions. To thaw one, reinvent it as a destination for a favorite activity; think about anything you and your family enjoy doing and build it into your home. A TV can be an integral part of the room, but unless you're turning the space into a home theater, it shouldn't be the primary focus; if it is, your furniture placement will forever be "off." If the room is large, divide it into zones: put a cozy sofa grouping in one corner where you can read or curl up to watch your favorite programs, while at the opposite end place a table for children's art projects. Line the walls with bookshelves filled with vintage paperback spy thrillers or anthologies of vintage comics, create a music corner stocked with a turntable and vinyl LPs, add chess and backgammon tables, or even a pool table, cocktail cabinet, or drum set. The possibilities are unlimited; the art comes in choreographing all of them in a fun and fresh new space.

(opposite, top and bottom) Endless sea meets infinite expanse of sky somewhere in a color field canvas by Donald Kaufman; the tension created by its interacting areas of color informed the choice of softly muted driftwood lavenders, grays, and blues. Thanks to that tempered palette, modern and classic styles can be juxtaposed without creating a jarring effect. The elegant proportions and exquisite detailing of the more traditional armchairs pair beautifully with a sleek, one-of-a-kind Aldo Tura scrolled-leg waterfall table covered in lacquered parchment.

Equally adjustable and movable furniture is essential in these multitasking rooms to avoid the spatial limitations that come with fixed objects. (There really should be a monument somewhere to Seibert Chesnutt, the unsung genius who invented the swivel caster!) Don't be afraid to move things into the center of the room if that will help the space come alive. Sectional sofas enable versatility and creativity with seating arrangements, and nothing says relaxation and ease like a chaise longue or daybed—they're excellent for afternoon catnaps as well as accommodating any overnight campers. Nesting tables and large upholstered ottomans that can double as coffee tables are standard design solutions, but my particular favorite, the *demilune*, or half-moon table, is probably the most versatile. Keep a pair of these beauties in an entry hall; if you need to seat a few more people at a dinner party, put one at either end of the table and you'll instantly have room for those extra guests.

Most interior designers turn their living rooms into showpieces, but in my home, I had one right off the entry that nobody ever used. It was too far from the kitchen, and since it was quite large, it would have cost a fortune to furnish. At the time, my kids had a vibrant blue Ping-Pong table in the garden; they played all the time and hated to have to stop at sunset. For my part, I didn't want what was prime real estate in the house to go unused—so I brought the Ping-Pong table into the living room. It certainly made a statement, but giving it a significant black paint scheme allowed the room to hold its own with the rest of the house. The contrast looked and felt so edgy and rock 'n' roll that I added their guitars and amps. The boys are older now, but they used to spend countless hours in that room. You have to be flexible in your approach to challenges like this and think about what your life needs are, rather than what is conventional and expected. It's actually a wonderful concept to have spaces in a home that can't be defined by conventional names.

(*opposite and following spread*) When you live in a temperate climate you always want to throw open all the doors and windows and to draw it in. The quality of light in this delightful poolside living room entranced me from the start, so I used pale finishes and elegant Gustavian elements to capture that lighter-than-a-feather, floating, breathless effect. I love the folly of this elaborate table skirt next to the light and breezy shape of the neoclassical chair. On their own these pieces are elegant and even regal, but something in their pairing is so relaxed that you could be barefoot and still feel entirely at home in this garden-like retreat.

There are so many modern elements that co-exist beautifully with more classic pieces. Furniture should never look like it landed from another planet.

The empty or "negative" space that's allowed to surround an object is just as important as the object itself. Accentuating that balance means that the clean, strong geometrics in this space—the A-frame supports, the perfect sphere of the coffee urn, the perpendicular lines of the lattice, the flat plane of the table, the curve of the chair arms—all become more emphatic.

(*following spread*) Back in the post-atomic 1950s, a vision of what the space-age future would look like was characterized by two chairs: the Swan and the Egg. While we aren't the Jetsons yet, these timeless classics of modernist industrial design have struck out on their own, claiming territory in both contemporary and traditional rooms. The welcoming, half-open wings of one invite you to sit among their embracing curves; the other beckons you into an enfolding cocoon. Reinterpreted in a soft watercolor palette, their fluid lines and organic shapes contrast pleasingly with the more structured and angular elements of the room. Underneath it all, the raised Greek key pattern in the rug is a nod to the foundation of traditional classic design.

My formal living room became a game room, a music room, and a hub of other family activity—and had yet another identity up its sleeve for large-scale entertaining.

How you should entertain is a reflection of how you should decorate—utterly sophisticated yet completely relaxed. Once you move the party into a kitchen, hallway, or library everyone's attitude becomes liberated; conversation is that much more relaxed and intimate without that "formal room" constraint. I actually configured my kitchen so company could be served directly from the stovetops; it creates a kind of foodie choreography and a wonderful collaborative dynamic between me and my guests. Entertaining is all about laughter, food, family, and friends, and providing a creative and elegant setting for all of them to come together.

(*following spread*) I love the blue of this oversize Ping-Pong table—it's an exclamation point that draws your eye to the center of the room. Once it took up residence along with my sons' guitars, the challenge was how to present that edgy diversity. I used a bone black flat finish for the walls, gloss for the millwork, and a cool, sleek white for the fireplace stones and crown moldings. Black stretches the perimeter—add an ebony sisal rug, and the lines of the room disappear. Everything floats and the space seems boundless.

I'm like an unruly child when it comes to design. There's always a point where I say: "What if this weren't the dining room?"

(*previous spread*) Paint a kitchen a sophisticated and dramatic shade like navy or charcoal—and you'll transform it into a space that is handsome by day and glamorous by night. Our midnight blue kitchen has beautiful paneling, elegant hardware, marble floors and countertops, mercury-glass backsplashes, and chandeliers hanging from a white tin ceiling. I really wanted an "Is it an industrial kitchen or an elegant paneled library?" back-and-forth shift, so open shelving holds a collection of books next to crystal, silver, and all-white porcelain. It's the most beautiful room in the house, and we do all our living—and entertaining—in this space because everyone wants to be here!

One thing that really resonated with me during my shopping raids in France was the wonderful metal shelving in the bakeries and pastry shops. Okay, it might've been partly due to the meringues they were holding up, but I'm pretty darn sure it was the displays themselves—there was a wonderful architectural feel to those graceful towers that seemed to be missing in other industrial stack-'em-ups. These blackened-patina metal units with arched supports, marble shelves, and mirrored backings, combined with the polished-nickel scale, transform this kitchen alcove into a little corner of Paris.

54321 History and Fundamentals
Techniques and Equipment
Animals and Plants
Ingredients and Preparations
Plated-Dish Recipes

(*above*) Appreciating the past and maintaining a physical connection to it is an important aspect of design—many reclaimed elements, like these heavily studded and hand-carved doors salvaged from a pair of Spanish *estancia* gates, were incorporated into this home. Aged patinas add to the richness and warmth of the colors and textures in the natural building elements and give the house an organic attachment to the landscape around it.

(*previous spread and opposite*) Raising ceilings, enlarging doorways and adding this expansive loft like kitchen and family area opened up the house and completely changed its energy. The huge cage-door windows give the owners an immediate connection to the stunning scenery that surrounds their home, so they feel as though they're living in the midst of the paddock, stables and newly planted vineyard.

I love the particularly
European sensibility
that comes when a new
generation infuses an
ancestral home with their
modern way of life.

Serious shelving in these floor-to-ceiling bookcases emphasizes the vertical aspect of
a room and gives the space a unified, seamless look. Painting the back of the shelves
adds depth and lets the rainbow colors of your books appeal to the eye. For a change,
rock covers paper as marble sculptures and metal ornamentation break up the space.
Bronze trumpet lights make it easier to find your favorite read; the hard choice
is whether to relax on the pale agate blue bench-seat sofa or sink into the antique
wingback leather chair. Nothing loves a library more than leather; new stylized,
contemporary open barrel-back chairs grouped around the table make up the set.

Children really can be seen *and* heard if there's a space like this: an art table with kid-proportioned seating, oodles of crayons and other art supplies wrangled into jars and wicker baskets, and a ladder so parents or children can grab a book from the shelves. The mother of these free-range moppets appreciated her desk placed on the other side of the sofa: it gives her an area of her own, yet allows her to oversee the fun without cramping anyone's style.

I like to include a style
wildcard in every
room—something
that complements the
other pieces in the
room, yet really stands
up and is noticed.

This turn-of-the-century neo-Georgian house easily lent itself to interesting contemporary pieces and a more modern color scheme without surrendering its original lines. In the days before central heating, the fireplace took center stage; the flattened ogee-style arch of this original mantel is still the focus of the room, and its architectural styling works beautifully with the curved cutouts in the geometric étagère tower. The deep mid-century modern lounge chair picks up that angular line and pays it forward.

(*following spread*) In a multistory house, the family room is generally on the first floor—but it's always important to let lifestyle win out over the floor plan. The wide age range of the family's children meant that as the little ones' bedtime approached, their elder siblings would still be up and about—so I converted this balconied, octagonal-shaped sitting area right off the master bedroom into an indoor/outdoor family room extraordinaire. Its central location makes it a natural gathering place as the household migrates upstairs when evening falls. They end their day as a family unit, enjoying that last important bit of playtime or just-one-more-chapter right before bed.

ARTBEAT ANOTHER LONEL
T STILL GRACEFUL
MILIAR REPLACED NOW
ERE IS A FACE BUT ITS OF
CE MY BLURRY EYES ARE
R YOUR BLURRY EYES YET
OICE IS ALWAYS WITH ME
IGHT HERE WITH ME I NEE
OMETHING TELL ME YOU
I LOVE YOU AGAIN ASK ME
Y THE SILENCE NOW TAL
AT ME ANYTHING TO ME I
G LEFT NO DREAM ALL
GERS THE DROWNING SOUN
GING VOICE TELL ME YOU
LOVE ME I AM NOT LIKE
EE I AM SCARED LO
T HEARTBEAT HEAR

One of the first things I did when we moved into this house was break through the walls so I could link these separate spaces together: this enfilade, or the long view of a room beyond a room beyond a room, gives true depth to decorating. The living room transitioning into the sitting area and then the kitchen is infinitely appealing. Despite the different activities that go on in each space, they're now linked together through this series of doorways, and will never feel too far apart or disconnected. Soon after the dust settled, the former owner came by for a cup of coffee and a look-see, and declared that if he knew the house could have looked like this, he never would have sold it!

Repurposing an entryway for large-scale entertaining is actually a modern take on the medieval "dining hall," which was a multifunction room large enough to seat the whole household.

Providing flattering light for your guests in the entryway is the icing on the cake of a great arrival experience—and in a multipurpose space, it really pays off. For any entertainment, the series of chandeliers in this spacious entry hallway provides elegant illumination—on a low dimmer, all the silver and crystal sparkles. It's the perfect ambiance—your guests will feel relaxed and want to linger for hours.

(*above and opposite*) The cutout fretwork of this old garden bench plays off the intricate design of the tile in this Old Hollywood home. It's a perfect bridge to the outside world that lies just beyond the front door; the firewood stacked underneath heightens the rustic feel. I took that geometric, interlocking motif into the adjacent breakfast nook, and couldn't resist adding the delightful image of the polar bear standing guard on his classically patterned black-and-white tile floor—now that's an outside element staking a claim!

Equestrian design
elements celebrate a unique
combination of grace and
power. Displaying horse
brasses, trophies, ribbons,
or boots shouldn't
be limited to the barn.

There's nothing like a horse barn for contrasts: they abound with rich textiles; iron,
brass and silver metals; supple leathers; and painted wood. It's a natural setting in
which to incorporate antique hardware, lighting, and, wherever possible, display all
of the evidence of a life well lived. This tack room could revitalize any centuries-old
European hunting lodge: the stylish display of antlers, hunting cups, boots, and
gleaming plated finishes is an homage to the life—and love—of a sport.

(*following spread*) You'd never believe this hilltop ranch and vineyard is only a few
miles from Malibu Beach—the scenery is too gorgeous not to make full use of every
inch! A connection to history isn't limited to architecture and décor—by placing
"inside" elements in an outdoor setting, the living area is extended into the welcoming, dappled light underneath a huge 200-year-old pine tree, With the addition of
these deeply padded armchairs slipcovered in natural-weave fabrics, an otherwise
prosaic patio setting is transformed into something unexpected and extraordinary.

(*opposite and above*) As horse owners will tell you, their barns are actual living spaces that reflect their passion for the equine life, so what children who live and breathe horses wouldn't spend every waking moment with them if they could? The studio space in the upper level of this stable is a perfect hangout; the half-circle window arch fills the aerie with an amazing light during the day; the intricate sunburst fixture provides welcoming illumination at night. (As if that weren't enough versatility, the barn sits atop a cutaway multibay garage that houses another kind of "horsepower"—a collection of vintage cars.) The exposed beams, natural wood planking, stone floor, and metal fixtures resonated with everyone; the parents demanded a retreat on the ground floor because they weren't going to let the kids have all the fun! It's a toss-up as to who loves this unique arrangement more—the horses or the family.

Everything should feel like it's of the present, but with some kind of connection to the past. Even a breakfast room needs to have some history in it.

(*opposite, following spread*) The pattern of exposed beams and soaring ceiling height made this multipurpose great room exciting—and a real challenge. The goal was to emphasize that "loft" feel, but since the height of the space could easily dwarf everything, a solid visual anchor at the end of the room was needed to ground it and make the space manageable. There was enough of this reclaimed antique firebrick from Belgium to construct a towering fireplace wall all the way to the top; the whitewashed patina looks as if the wall had been plastered over long ago and then eroded away with age. That sense of texture is the defining note; a spontaneous grouping of mismatched chairs, gathered like historic driftwood around the table, adds to the eclectic feel of the space. The light, soft palette of pale blues, grays, lavenders, and whites harmonizes with the gardens beyond the double French doors.

(*above and opposite*) In a multifunctional, layered space like this, no one has to leave and attend to other aspects of their lives if they don't wish to. There are so many interlocking patterns present in this space—the beams, the brickwork, the honeycomb on the fireplace-seat upholstery, the lines in the rug. They all symbolize an interconnectedness and underlying framework that families possess—exactly what I want to enable and reinforce through design.

(*following spread*) A series of gardens encompasses the house; thanks to wide French doors scattered throughout, the family has a seamless connection to ever-changing nature. All that was missing to complete the experience was an alfresco dining space. The addition of this rustic, vine-draped pergola right off the kitchen area provides cool shade and creates the ultimate morning room. Beautiful weather-resistant teak benches and a farmhouse table add a lively dimension by providing fun picnic-style seating.

Just as your jewelry shouldn't be too "matchy-matchy," the same goes for hardware finishes in your kitchen—mixing metals can be just as satisfying as mixing colors. The warm, rich gold tones of brass drop chandeliers and the faucet pop in contrast with the cool nickel and stainless steel. I have a special fondness for the range hood: the unexpected decoratively bound edges and strap detailing call to mind an old-fashioned portmanteau-type suitcase or luxury traveling trunk.

(*following spread*) Diverse styles in a shared space don't have to be boring to play nicely together. The kitchen is home to that rebel of the design world: the minimalist industrial style. Stripped down and agleam with metal, it commands both functionality and luxe finished details. The dividing arch element has a unique textural note that can really hold its own against that steel-clad bad boy; the pin-tuck effect of the ceiling and soffit creates a more rustic look that provides the perfect setting for the relaxed California-casual sitting area.

Design doesn't just end at the front door; interior and exterior elements should flow seamlessly across your threshold.

If you have to look twice to realize that there are no glass walls surrounding this laid-back living room space, that's as it should be. While topiaries, treillage, and other garden architectural features are a delightful way to bring the outside footprint indoors, don't stop there. The relaxed conversational grouping of tropical bamboo chairs with their blackened-bronze stain blend perfectly with other raw and weathered materials that claim this original and transitional space.

124

A SENSE OF COLOR

I was an unabashed color junkie from an early age. In my part of Kansas, it seemed like everything that wasn't wheat, corn, or a rusted-out tractor was dirt-colored. I desperately craved pure, clear color and considered it a tragedy that my footie pajamas from the Sears Roebuck catalog didn't come in chartreuse or lavender. There was nothing more soothing to me than the contrast of a green treetop against blue sky, which is probably why I prefer the cooler end of the spectrum—blues, grays, and greens—to this day.

Color is the perfect, and also the most effortless, way to bring a subliminal order and connection into the home. Consider your home's physical layout when choosing your palette and pay attention to how natural light progresses through it during the day, since that will affect the tone and intensity of your colors. When deciding on a room's palette, look beyond its four walls: the color scheme should not only relate to the adjoining spaces, but to what's outside the windows. Colors in a garden, koi pond, or lush landscape can inspire the hue of the upholstery in the living room or the painted backs of the bookshelves in the library.

If you keep colors restricted to five or less, they can be repeated throughout your design, creating a cohesive look between rooms. By using a particular hue on the walls in one room, on the trim in another, and then again in an ottoman fabric or Roman shade, you will create a pleasing connection and a sense of rhythm, as well as a continuous thread running throughout your home that will unify the space.

Don't be afraid to stop at the walls: consider your floors and the ceilings as well. Natural wood brings its own organic color to a room, but a painted floor can be a revitalizing element. Back when the sterile white kitchen was en vogue, I momentarily horrified a client by painting her kitchen floorboards bright blue. That pop of color transformed the space from an operating theater to a

room that was welcoming and evocative of the farmhouse kitchen. She was initially apprehensive—not about the color, but about walking on it. "What if it wears? What if we damage it?" I replied, "Good!" And meant it. Painted floors, worn by use and full of cracks, add a wonderfully provincial element to any space; they pull people into a room in the way a pristine "hands off" finish never can. They can also be a clever method of introducing a pattern, or bringing an "outside" color right across the threshold and into the home, in a way that might otherwise be too overwhelming or obvious.

Ceilings can do amazing things when paired with the right hue; if they're textured or patterned, color is going to bring out that surface in a wonderful and unexpected way. Tin ceilings painted in a bold or luminous color can transform a space into a real gem, putting the lid on what can become a real jewel box of a room.

Blues and grays are mercurial and mystical, bringing a calming and spiritual sensuality into a room, and when taken to clear, transparent water tints, become an alluring embodiment of silver. Confident, optimistic colors like pinks and oranges are vibrant and energizing, creating an intriguing and memorable impression, especially when paired together. Reds can energize and invigorate any space: whether playful and warm, or serious and dramatic, they always make an impressive statement. Greens and yellows are fresh and earthy; they invigorate and add a smart "country-club" feel to any space. Browns, taupes, and purples can be both relaxing and intense, adding a deep and serious classic note; blacks and deep navy or indigo blues bring a bold, strong sophistication in a more classic manner.

As Elsie de Wolfe knew, beiges and creams are clean and peaceful; they relax the eye, envelope the senses, and create a cohesive look between rooms. They're universal, timeless colors and bring a sense of order and classic appeal to a space, especially when combined with natural wood.

(*previous spread*) Sometimes if you let the plot go, a color story can end up writing itself. This lovely saturated orchid color was for a magazine shoot. After the photographers left, I covered the sofa with this gorgeous turquoise and white tapestry, added a saffron-colored armchair—and I was suddenly transported to Jaipur! The color is so vital that I realized anything could go here; the more I added to the space, the more it bloomed. It's incredibly satisfying to put colors and textures together like this and see the synergy that results.

I've been collecting antique fabrics for years: to upholster this lounge chair for my bedroom I combined vintage Indian embroidery in ambers and ruby reds with a newer gold-and-white-striped material. The blend of subtle textures and array of colors made the project wildly successful, with each piece of fabric enhancing the effect of the other. Whether your interior is modern or traditional, a pillow made from a sari, kuba cloth, or embroidered suzani will create a worldly feel. "Found" textiles will not only stand the test of time, they are a lovely and tangible link to the past.

Using slightly different tones of stark white or cream makes a room a perfect canvas and gives it a layered depth, while using different textures like fleece, fur, silk burlap, or suede, and mixing luxurious or nubby patterns like burnout, jacquard, herringbone, or basket weave, creates amazing depth that throws the space into dramatic high relief. Add sleek, glossy finishes like lacquer and polished stone, and the room will resonate in subtle and wonderful ways.

When de Wolfe started a design revolt by painting over the dark Victorian paneling of her day in white and cream, black was still thought to be unsuitable as a decorating color—if it was used at all, it was reserved for accents. For years people were advised to avoid it because the color would be "depressing" or "shrink" the room, so much so that the rebellious teenager who wants to paint his or her room black over the horrified parents' objections has become a classic trope in film and comics. (My sons' bedroom was painted black well before they reached that stage—it was the perfect background for their Iggy Pop posters and sports paraphernalia. Thankfully it never occurred to them to be really perverse and demand white walls instead!)

My own fascination with black dates back to when I got my first pair of tap shoes. It symbolized strength and functionality for me back then, and I'm thrilled to see that many are adopting a more progressive color attitude. Ebony herringbone marble for a kitchen backsplash, contrasted with glossy white sinks, snowy tile, and creamy marble with nickel fixtures, is at once arrestingly fresh, powerful, and timeless. It will create an unexpected depth to a small space when used with white mortar on the floor of a butler's pantry; take that idea a step further with caviar-colored leather on a closet floor to create a dark, sophisticated mood. Black barware and decanters with silver spouts will make your champagne even more special, and jet glass and crystal on light fixtures proves that there's a flip side to every classic.

For me, it's not about creating a signature color or utilizing a palette of my own, but in working to create a color story and design rationale that speaks to my clients and that they can feel passionate about.

Fashion photographs like this Mark Shaw print from the 1950s are always an inspiration; the appealing grace notes of orange in the iconic Hermès boxes are echoed by the luscious cashmere throw in the next room. Edgy and sophisticated design can turn a room into a vibrant space that people want to be in; it's through color that you can adjust that volume.

Visiting Elizabeth Taylor's home, I was struck by the colors she used to enhance the beauty of those legendary violet eyes. No wonder Richard Burton married her twice!

I've decorated my table for years with violets in silver trophy cups, but the day I visited Elizabeth Taylor's home it was like rediscovering the color all over again. Every Easter my grandmother would make dresses for my sister and me—we'd choose a color and go through the McCall's pattern book for just the right style. To this day I remember her laying tissue paper patterns over that carefully selected fabric; I recall the delicate pins in a neat little row. Then one year, after so many pinks and yellows and greens, a bolt of lavender voile caught my eye . . .

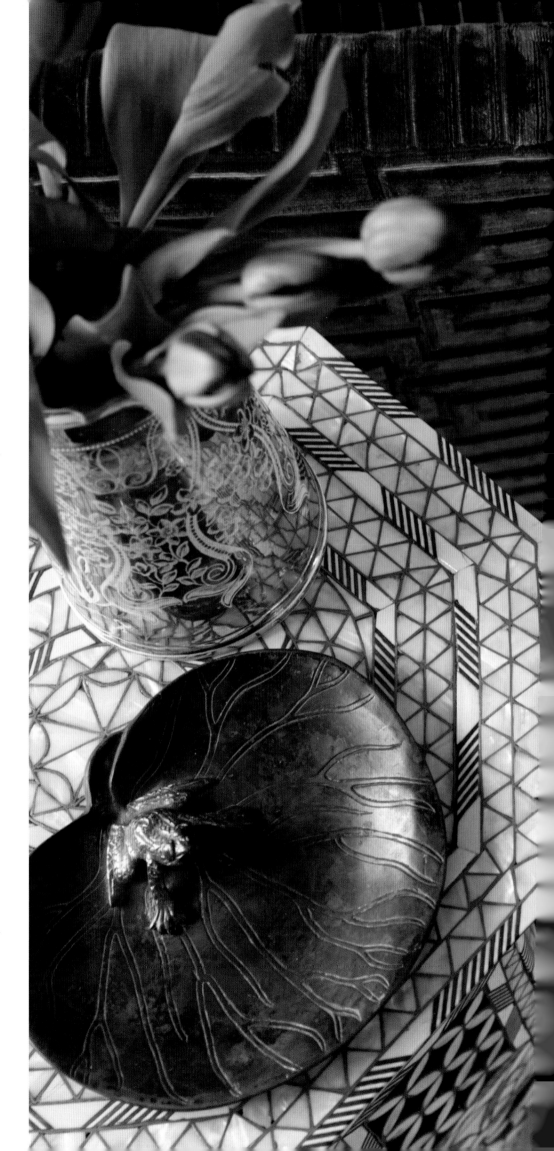

(*previous spread*) Rumored to have been built by Charlie Chaplin for a paramour, this Spanish Colonial-style villa embodies the enormous influence the early film industry had on revival architecture in the 1920s. Movies set in exotic locales popularized a wide range of styles—a mix of miniature Spanish haciendas, Tudor manses, and Cape Cod cottages—that quickly took California beyond the classic bungalow. Silent film star Mary Pickford—no friend of Chaplin's—condemned this style mixing as vulgar, but even she would approve of this breezy, open-arched room. It's an intimate space that makes a big statement: the antique sunburst over the fireplace introduces a rich note of old gold; the period triangular-winged griffin chandelier firmly tethers the space to its unique and historic past.

Fit for Old Hollywood royalty, a deeply saturated palette of rich sapphire blues and amethyst violets sets the stage. A geometric collaboration of the intricate upholstery design and the facets outlined in the rug mesh seamlessly with the tone-on-tone pattern on the king-of-beasts claw-foot ottoman. The opalescent mosaic tiles in the octagonal Moroccan table lift that interlocking tracery to yet another dimension.

Diana Vreeland's observation that "pink is the navy blue of India" is a delightful notion—I love the idea that there's a spot on earth where it's that commonplace.

This master bedroom suite has all the romantic sophistication of a Paris salon crossed with the grace and elegance of a Gatsby-era Palm Beach country club. It all started with the freestanding *bibliothèque*: its distinctive metal fretwork was so fascinating that I built the room around it. That stylized, interconnected motif runs from the custom rug to the paneled ceiling, and I chose the square triple-tiered chandelier from the 1920s to highlight the effect. When I proposed a pale palette—blush pink with taupe accents—for the room, I was delighted to discover that far from being threatened by the notion, the husband loved his sorbet-colored, pastel golf shirts and trousers!

(*following spread*) Until the end of the Second World War, pink was actually considered a "masculine" color—since it was so close to red, it was decreed to be stronger and more "decided" than blue, which was deemed wishy-washy and therefore perfect for little girls! While we've thankfully come a long way from having to follow the dictates of gender-specific colors, one way to overcome any lingering objections to this oh-so-flattering hue is to restrict its use to harder-edged and restrained forms.

Renoir spent forty years discovering that "the queen of all colors is black." She has always enjoyed an uninterrupted reign in whatever home I've lived in.

(*previous spread*) California bungalow meets New England cottage in this home-office refuge. The blooming lotus on the softly hued wallpaper frames the garden view; contemporary touches like a lacquered secretary and sinuous metal-supported chair keep the room from becoming too sweet—or simple. Open windows are encouraged, as the chandelier was converted from a wind chime; its melodic zinc "coins" contrast with the blackened-bronze sconces, ladder rail, and high-luster gold furniture finishes.

A fruitwood chest or other piece of campaign furniture never shows to better advantage than when it's displayed against black, and a gilt mirror will never have a better friend than an ebony wall. Dense hues of black depend on under-tones of red, blue, or brown for their drama and intensity, making them a designer's delight to work with. It's calming, smart, and sophisticated, especially when combined with large doses of white linen and great architectural elements.

This unused, dark-paneled breakfast room took on a new life as an entertainment setting—it's perfect for intimate dinner parties. The raised detail in the paneling inspired the medallions in the white coffered ceilings and the string of studs at the base of the deep, sapphire-blue velvet chairs. I quite literally put a contemporary spin underneath this classic setting with a custom Chinese silk rug in a linked border motif.

(*following spread*) Natural materials pack an abundance of color all on their own: wooden floors will glow in a warm wash of sunlight, silver will acquire a soft patina over time, bright copper will oxidize to lovely greens and blues. The blackened-bronze planter and Balinese rain drums set the beat for an ethnically textured and worldly room: an ikat-style textile hints of India; the heavily chased silver escutcheons on the mirror frame add a Moroccan note; and the silk tribal print at the mullioned window brings the lovely melody together.

I prefer to use hues at the warm end of the spectrum as accents. "Pops" of intense color bring a room to life; they can be far more effective than an overall wash of pigment.

When a client told me, "I come from a red place," I decided to illustrate the kitchen. Lacquered cherry-red Chinese Chippendale dining chairs cluster around the breakfast table underneath a whimsical crimson metal pagoda lantern; a poppy-colored linen lampshade tops off the center island. Apart from a scarlet-corded tree swing in the garden outside, that was it. With the strategic placement of a few bold strokes, my client had the lasting impression she was surrounded by her favorite color.

This Spanish Colonial Revival residence is the epitome of Silent Era Hollywood glamour. The dreamy nostalgia for the days when Rudolph Valentino could say it all with just his eyes is still an integral component of design in Los Angeles. It inspired the deeply saturated slate and indigo blues offset by equally lush garnet and crimson accents. The heavily patterned and textured neutrals provide a rich and luxurious counterpoint.

Curtains, walls, and furnishings in the same patterned fabric is quintessentially English. The look is delightful and calming, which is why these rooms have long been among my favorites.

Little ones don't stay that way for long, so a "theme" bedroom that suits their younger fantasies needs to be attractive and imaginative enough to keep up with their stylistic growth spurts. It doesn't have to come down to a choice between superheroes or unicorns: this striking paisley-chintz bedroom is fit for a long-ago-and-far-away Indian princess, but will delight the dreams of any modern western tween. Girly yet grown-up, playful yet sophisticated, it's an enchanting vision that will inspire for years to come. The vintage iron bedstead, antique English lantern chandelier, and white leather ottoman complete the appealing picture.

Whether it's a tuxedo or this silk-velvet sofa, there's a special romance attached to midnight blue. The trend-setting Duke of Windsor popularized this deepest, most saturated shade as an alternative for traditional black formalwear in the 1920s, realizing that the spectrum-shifting photogenic properties of indigo blue would allow the new medium of black-and-white press photography to record subtle tailoring details. This wonderful chameleon color works its exotic magic just as well in décor; here its rich depth is used in both paint and fabric to transform this tone-on-tone room into a dramatic and intensely elegant setting.

159

(*opposite*) From palest blue-gray to robin's egg, aqua is one of my cool and elegant favorites—and a perfect choice for these pierced-arm mid-century lounge chairs, since it was a defining design color for the 1950s. A table with whimsical heron bird feet was a delightfully natural pairing with this "water" color—all that's missing is a tray of caviar to complete the elemental theme! (*above*) I had the same fun with this modernist chair from the same era in my dressing room. I fell in love with the frame, so to make the most of it I had it replated in matte gold, then reupholstered the seat and back in a luxurious silvery leather. Every piece of clothing I own looks wonderful draped across it!

Don't be afraid to use black, deep navy, and charcoal as basic colors; balance them with large doses of white for a sophisticated and dramatic effect.

Colorful canvases, graphics, or photographs always show to advantage on a black wall; displaying monochromatic art in the same space yields a really special result. The focus of the eye shifts within the color of the artwork, honing in on the purity of texture and surface detail. The warm undertones of the lampblack basket-weave wall finish enhances the cool tones of the panoramic image in this cosmopolitan Manhattan apartment.

(*following spread*) Chanel's observation that "simplicity is the keynote of all true elegance" informs the color scheme in this modernist high-rise pied-à-terre. While its color scheme is a restrained palette of charcoals and neutrals, the nuances of texture and complex pattern notes in the variegated silk rug, wall covering, and fabrics give the contemporary space a cool, urbane sophistication and unusual visual depth.

This shaded outdoor living room in the poolhouse next to our tennis court and koi pond is a welcome refuge from the sun by day, and a glowing entertainment pavilion by night as a pop-down screen transforms the space into a modern, sophisticated version of the drive-in movie theater. Classic awning stripes add a beachy, resort feel; I adore the clean contrast with the herringbone pattern in the natural stone floor and fireplace. The bead-be-decked statues stand guard over the family space—and what better place for modern gargoyles than an outdoor temple?

(*following spread*) This spacious, all-white open kitchen area is agleam with subway-tile flooring and white-and-dark-chocolate-swirl marble countertops. The wash of strong light accentuates the custom-fluted walls so that they're reminiscent of the starched folds in a chef's toque—or is it the beautifully pressed pleats of a fine lawn tuxedo shirt? An oval wooden table with pillarlike white legs and foot rail doubles as a prep island; it stands at counter height so that guests can easily gather around it and sample whatever's hot off the stove.

CONNECTING PAST & PRESENT

radition holds an incredible allure for me, probably because I didn't grow up with a lot of it. My people were pioneers and independent adventure types, so while my maverick chromosomes respond to classic themes, they're ones that are realized through today's sensibilities, infused with contemporary elements.

Giving the old a new perspective is critical to good design, but so is imparting a sense of history to the new. If I'm in a room where everything is raw, featureless, and brand-new, I feel either uncomfortable or disappointed, as if I've arrived too late to the party. I want a story, to be surrounded by things that hold a vibration and note of history.

It's important for every space to have a piece with a provenance; even a breakfast room needs to have some history in it. Your home doesn't have to look as if you ransacked the finds of an entire episode of *Antiques Roadshow*—rustic, reclaimed and vintage pieces, and architectural elements also honor the past while adding interest to the present. Every space that I design mixes the past and the present to varying degrees, but all too often, the impression is that decorating with antiques will result in a really stuffy version of your least-favorite grandma's house—with doilies. That couldn't be more wrong, as there's a special romance to a room where the objects in it have a heritage. Not only is it an intriguing notion that something far older than you has managed to survive wars, depressions, all sorts of upheavals, and ownership by numerous people (with stories of their own!), but its continued existence is often due solely to a level of craftsman-ship that is rarely seen nowadays. Even in a casual setting, layering vintage or heirloom pieces with more contemporary design elements is not only visually pleasing, it's an important way for people to relate to the past without having to sacrifice a connection to the present.

A room that's devoted to just one time period—whether it's antique or modern—runs the risk of looking like a movie set, while an eclectic interior that crosses all sorts of style and era boundaries, such as combining a Directoire writing desk with a mid-century Scandinavian wingback chair and mirrored lamps, is the sort of diverse mix that makes a room unique. There are subtle tricks for blending the past and the present: in a family room with contemporary upholstered furniture, include a formal element like a Louis XV settee with a carved wood frame and cabriole legs—and then add a couple of deep, wide lounge chairs that you can really sink into. Variations of this "antiques and armchairs" unconventional pairing of old and new always feels vital and exciting.

Weaving the past with the present often involves a sort of restoration. Reintroducing the older concept of purposed rooms back into today's pattern of living is one way to reinstate that link to tradition and the past—"updating" an older piece is yet another. Something as simple as slip-covering antique settees in a light, pared-down fabric, such as Belgian linen or seersucker, can bring fresh air into a room, but sometimes more is required. Ever since I started bringing classic furniture and architectural elements back from Europe, one of my favorite tricks has been to take a wood cabinet with classic lines or intricate fretwork and paint it. Applying white or indigo lacquer to a classic shape brings a fresh, contemporary look to the piece, and gives timeless elegance a head-turning twist—it's amazing how a color that's "now" will make it a transforming element. Breaking the "rules" is sometimes the best way to enhance the story.

(previous spread) "Humble yet royal" is an apt description of the Gustavian look, an eighteenth-century fusion of Swedish restraint and neoclassical styling. Characterized by a cool color story utilizing pale, light-reflective surfaces to combat the long, dark Scandinavian winter, its elegant lines and stark simplicity suit the classically restrained proportions of this older Hudson Valley country estate—the view in the towering carved pier glass could easily be of Stockholm, Lake Zurich, or other romantic European retreat.

Minimalism has its roots in architecture and design; part of its unique allure is using only truly essential elements and letting calm, bold lines and pure forms speak for themselves. You don't need to pile on details or objects for their own sake; it's through simplicity that you'll achieve true sophistication and refinement in design.

Resistance is futile when it comes to responding to the lines and silhouettes in this light-filled room. The elegant arch of the windows and curves of the Biedermeier-style sofa are echoed in the sinuous arabesque of the whimsical camels' necks and the horns of the antelope bust—they all inject a playful note that prevents the space from being too austere.

While writing your own history in your homefront, never be shy about displaying prized possessions that have special meaning. So often the smallest thing, such as a piece of blue and white porcelain, can inspire the design or color scheme of an entire room—and give it a uniquely personalized point of view. Inspiration for that narrative can come from anywhere: a gorgeous crystal chandelier, a collection of mechanical instruments, a wooden yacht model, a family portrait, the most costly Oriental rug, or an inexpensive garage sale treasure—as long as it's important to you. One client who was an inveterate reader had stumbled upon an old diary hidden in a pile of old books at a flea market. The book was probably about eighty years old and in it the unknown author described a passionate love affair. What better place for it than the library? I found an amazing chandelier and had dozens of its tiny lampshades covered in the diary's handwritten pages. In this way, the love story was illuminated—and the room looked smashing.

There's nothing like a well-traveled house, with rooms that have true personality created by objects that seem to have been carefully accumulated over time. For that reason, I've always been drawn to the British style of decorating because it feels incredibly unselfconscious and natural, yet is still so richly layered in history. In the well-decorated English home, classical busts are more than likely to live alongside artifacts from the Far East or Indian Raj, in rooms with heirloom Axminster carpets covering the floor. Tables are set with silver and crystal. Furniture spans the centuries. I think this visual smorgasbord is one reason *Downton Abbey* struck such a popular chord—there's nothing quite like the notion of eating your Cheerios underneath a priceless tapestry or an ancestral portrait of the 17th Earl on horseback. I want to convey a sense of history, but one that's balanced with that sort of approachability. That's my design ideal when it comes to creating a timeless aesthetic.

A versatile pièce de résistance like this can make a room, such as this all-in-one secretaire-dressing table-étagère. Designer purses and jewelry have become legitimate art pieces (or so I recently told my husband when there was nothing in the till for an Ed Ruscha painting), and this little gem allows me the luxury of displaying my beloved collected-along-the-way handbags, bangles, and baubles as eye candy for my boudoir.

When there's no actual client and no obvious story to tell about a space, what do you do? When I'm at a loss for inspiration, a favorite trick is to imagine someone legendary in the space, so I decided to dream up a fantasy resident with a really interesting backstory. I really got into it and came up with a wacky idea: if the Duchess of Windsor and the Sultan of Brunei had a love child, this would be her room. This crazy premise and mash-up of sensibilities allowed me go wild. I designed a dramatic bed canopy— gorgeously pleated and tailored—inspired by the Duchess's soigné outfits. This was paired with a bed upholstered in zebra—a nod to the Sultan. The room was furnished with a Tony Duquette screen, a mother-of-pearl inlaid cabinet, pony-skin rug, and many other elegant treasures. It was an exotic rendezvous of east and west, old and new, past and present, his and hers—and glamorous as all get-out. Actually, forget the love child. When it was done, I wanted to move right in myself!

Giving the old a new perspective is critical to good design. The craftsmanship of pieces with a provenance makes them irresistible.

In the decades when men were the sole breadwinners and worked outside of the home, interior decoration was such a woman's domain that husbands almost needed a visa to gain entry. Now that roles are less defined, it's time for a stronger male representation in design spaces. There's a special synergy that comes from a strong yin/yang, masculine/feminine juxtaposition: these dominant hand-riveted repoussé trays from Spain with their heavy bronze patina absolutely resonate against the delicate silk-velvet-upholstered walls and ormolu sconces. Perfect foils enhance each other through that dynamic contrast—and like any good romantic pairing, that teamwork "whole" always ends up being greater than the sum of its parts.

(*following spread*) Avant-garde lighting choices and contemporary design forms are balanced against ornate furnishings and classic built-in cabinets in this bedroom suite. The richly ornate space revels in a riotous confluence of European, African, and Indian cultural elements, taking luxury to head-spinning new heights.

The Romans knew how to make a first—and often only—impression. Guests were received in the atrium in style, but only trusted friends had the privilege of being ushered into the rest of the house.

The entry to your home is the first room you see upon arrival and the last when you depart. It's the key to our personal worlds and sets the tone for what's in store, so don't just think prelude—think foreplay. This historic turn-of-the-century New York sporting estate retains its older exterior and presence, but opens up to show a layered and updated heart. Marbleized paper, cut into sections and turned, gives the impression of endpapers in an antique volume. The look is rich and nostalgic—almost theatrical—and arouses curiosity as to what lies beyond. No matter how casual we are in our everyday lives, everyone appreciates a great "reveal."

Abstract art in striking, bold colors is a great way to give an edge to a more traditional setting—in truth, it becomes a focal point no matter what the décor! Like many modern works, this James Nares canvas was meant to be displayed without a frame—it bursts off the wall without any limiting structure to confine it. The contrast with the ornate frames of the mirrors on either side heightens their intricate, tightly patterned curves while emphasizing the unrestrained free-form movement and vibrancy of this single crimson brushstroke.

I stole a vintage textile meant for my son's college apartment in a panic to upholster this ottoman—often it's an unplanned element that makes it all come together. I rely heavily on intuition— and divine intervention.

The shared spaces for multiple activities in this sunny room encourage the whole family to come together instead of just scattering after dinner or disappearing on the weekend. The mix of masculine and feminine elements in the floor-to-ceiling bookshelves, art table for projects, linen-slipcovered sectional sofas for comfortable conversation, and a leather-topped bar area for entertaining guests who've dropped by to watch a sports event appeal to everyone. It's a room where everyone can do his or her own thing at the same time, and yet still feel connected.

Incorporating older, reclaimed materials throughout gives the house character, patina, and imparts a sense of history. The distressed pair of Ionic pilasters emphasizes the height of the family-room ceiling and creates the feel of a domestic temple. For the final touch, antique firebricks from France were carefully divided so that there were enough to line the interiors of every fireplace in the house. It's that kind of design nuance that makes all the difference.

(above and opposite) What use is a work area if it's not gorgeous, fun, and inspiring? The Federalist farmhouse design effortlessly embraces these angular mid-century and retro classics; the beautifully formed, slender-profile gold-plated chairs that flank the stylized-sawhorse-supported art table inject a rich, worldly note that strikes a chord with the antique gilded mirror and this primitive burnished brass helmet. Their smooth and supple leather upholstery heightens the pleasing contrast with the wide, weathered natural-oak farmhouse planking.

Fretwork patterns are a
timeless way to unify classic
and contemporary elements.
They can be ornate or simple,
and I like to be unpredictable
about where I use them.

I love to use reclaimed architectural elements to give new construction a sense
of history. I found a pair of antique coffered ceilings that came out of an old
horse ranch in West Virginia and designed two rooms in this home around
them. They were covered in about ninety-four coats of paint, and they arrived
all jumbled together—the pieces had to be laid out in the courtyard and
reassembled like two gigantic jigsaw puzzles! But when all those paint layers
were stripped away, wonderful carved bosses and other detailing were revealed, so
that this library ceiling evokes the cover of a lovely carved wooden jewelry box.

(opposite and above) Go ahead and mix it up—a sense of history that's effortlessly balanced with modern approachability is particularly alluring. Of all the images you may see of beautiful rooms, how often do you get the impression that "this must be a family heirloom" or "that was collected along the way"? A space shouldn't look too contrived, but as though it has evolved naturally over time—along with all the little imperfections that contribute to making it feel "perfect" in the end. Timeless design as a part of everyday living—that's the feeling you want to capture.

Connecting with the
traditions of a bygone era can
be beneficial, since we
seem to have forgotten how
to slow down, relax,
and appreciate the civilized
comforts of life.

Whether it's backgammon, Risk, Go, or gin rummy—if you build it, they will come. There's a pleasing interaction that comes from layering libraries and game rooms; the contrast between the solitary inner pursuit of reading with the extroverted action of trying to best a competitor generates an interesting tension. I swear the space benefits from that lively back-and-forth shift in energy!

(*following spread*) Large-paned doors open up this expansive living room to light and the gorgeous vista outside. Without many tall architectural elements, a series of windows like this can put too much emphasis on the horizontal, especially when the roof pitch lines aren't particularly high. The floor-to-ceiling curtains break through that line: hung at the top of the wall, they pull the eye upward. The thinner, elegant rods add a touch of lightness and modernity in contrast with the room's more ornate fixtures.

(*above and opposite*) Leave debates over theory to the physicists and enjoy the lovely evidence that the passage of time leaves behind—namely, patina. An aged finish can be the result of amazing contradictions: decades of waxing and polishing can erode an object's surface just as years of neglect can add to it; sunlight, oxidation and other "natural" factors can damage it just as easily as careless accidents. The beautiful, mellow glow that an antique displays is a testament to its journey and survival through the years—it's a visual provenance, pedigree, and passport all rolled into one.

Since it was originally a formal dining room, this enticing billiards room is wonderfully accessible and smack in the middle of the ground floor—it's a far cry from the days when the catchall "rec room" used to be hidden away in the basement like a guilty secret. And while most homes have Wii or PlayStation and enough video games to sink a ship, the added benefit of having a dedicated recreation space like a music or game room is that if you have teenagers you won't need GPS to find them—chances are they'll be hanging out with their friends at your house!

Textiles can seamlessly integrate history into a space. Nothing tones down a "too perfect" or overly formal room like a slightly worn or frayed vintage fabric.

Fashion and interior design are like twin sisters that simply went to two different finishing schools—both are all about beauty and presentation, and, like siblings, each has a profound effect on the other. They both inform—and draw from—our collective consciousness; nothing can evoke a mood or specific point in history with more clarity than runway trends of tribal or animal prints, technicolor geometrics, or even vibrant tie-dye effects applied to walls and furnishings. Four centuries ago the novel beauty of imported floral-print cotton chintz wasn't just limited to clothing; unrestricted use of the same bolt of fabric for bed covers, walls, and curtains was a popular design choice. While the "all-over" effect in this dining room is still as fresh today as it was then, the updated version of a more rectangular block pattern on printed linen is a new—and almost architectural—way to use the power of florals.

(*above and opposite*) Whether it's a classically simple backless stool or more Baroque-style seating, decorative upholstery studs and nail heads elevate a construction necessity into an essential part of the design. They shouldn't be limited to furniture, either—they can make walls, screens, doors, or anything architectural into a transforming element. The bold corkscrew lines of the chair have an energy all their own; the intricate pattern of curls in the burnout fabric and the carpet play off that and emphasize the layered, rich-in-history feel of the space.

THE
HOME
IN
BALANCE

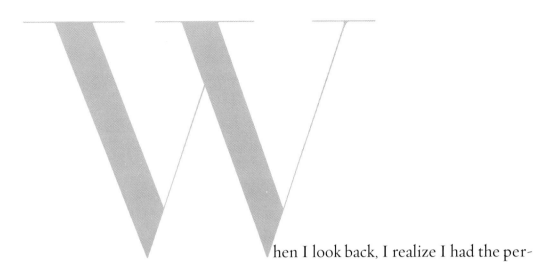

hen I look back, I realize I had the perfect education without even knowing it. Dancers have a daily discipline of exercising both sides of the brain as they learn to dance with both sides of the body, reversing all movements and repeating them so there is no weaker side. Just as holding a drawing up to a mirror will immediately reveal any flaws in its proportion and execution, the unique exercise of watching your dancing form in reverse trains your visual skills to identify what's "off," or not in line. That hyperdeveloped sense of balance means I see rooms and their contents as a series of lines: I can "walk" through them in my mind and know just how the spaces should flow, how the elements connect and overlap and support the design as a whole, and finally, what will enhance the "story" of the house and make it more compelling.

Designers often begin by asking: "What can I do to this room to make it gorgeous?" While that's a great end result for a static display, your home isn't a time capsule, nor does it exist in a vacuum. Truly successful rooms should not only reflect the life that's being lived in and around them, they should enhance it—and that means there needs to be a purpose behind any design choices. The real questions should be: "Where do you feel the happiest in your house? Where's the best sun in the morning? What are your hobbies?" It's the designer's role to really listen to how people aspire to live and then reclaim their home's best spaces, reimagining them to suit their hopes, dreams, and desires. Reinventing elegant and life-restoring spaces that are tailor-made for the people living in them will give the home that equilibrium and redefine its role in modern life.

Like a high-wire artist, a design needs to be in balance, but it should still be able to amaze and delight by performing an unexpected handspring. Balance means a house that nods to the past but doesn't feel enslaved by it. It's a living space that is at once elegant and refined, but also livable and comfortable. On a purely visual level, a home in balance engages all the senses without any single element feeling out of place. It's masculine and feminine, antique and modern, light and dark, austere and glam, rustic and sophisticated—all these things in perfect harmony.

While it's vital to design spaces that incorporate traditional architectural elements with more modern pieces, so is finding a balance of both of these worlds—the formal and the casual—in new combinations that feel right for today. An exuberant piece on the ornate side of the spectrum, like a coffee table with filigree or fretwork, selected to live beside a clean, modern piece like a streamlined sofa, is a perfect example of contrast—but more than that, it's one that will create a dynamic tension and a pleasing balance.

While the "opposites attract" type of counterpoint decorating makes everything livelier, a room needs to be well grounded to avoid a clash. Classical design principles such as symmetry and regularity of scale are essential to achieving visual harmony in a space. One of the easiest design tricks is the "Noah's Ark" principle: two by two. Whether it's a pair of matching armchairs in the living room, or identical pendant lamps at either end of a long table, the symmetry of pairs instantly conveys balance. Achieving that balance when it comes to scale is also crucial, as the size of the room dictates how large or small the furnishings should be.

Once the overall design plan has been established, then it comes down to the details. Again, "opposites attract" comes into play: if the wallpaper is metallic and sparkling, look for furnishings that provide a more organic and natural visual counterpoint, like wood or marble. If the armchairs appear slender and delicate, bring in an ample sofa with a deliberately chunky

Nothing can touch the visual impact of a glossy caviar-black leather chair and lustrous black doors in a creamy white hallway. Rather than distract from that perfect balance, why not literally reflect on it? I'm a Pisces, so water is an element I really respond to—shimmery, reflective, and wavering surfaces like this distressed mercury-glass-mirrored table is a big part of the look.

arm. Fine silks next to nubby Belgian linens, Carrara marble together with reclaimed wood—these textural combinations might not seem like obvious pairings, but put them together and they'll accentuate the best in each other—and in the process create a fission that will animate the entire space, making it a sumptuous feast for the eye.

It's actually easy to be over-the-top ornate or even gaudy; perfect simplicity and low-key elegance are the hardest things to achieve. If the room is in balance, when no one element is hollering "look at me!" and when the eye finds equilibrium, you'll more than know it—you'll feel it. That ebonized desk that's been in the family forever, that little sculpture that you bought at the arcade on King's Road, or that painting you snatched up at a garage sale—these things can all come to life and sing in harmony.

Every home needs rooms and corners where its residents can retreat and recharge. Quiet is the ultimate luxury nowadays, so it's vital to carve out spaces where people can work, read, reflect, or pursue an absorbing activity, whether it's chess or billiards. But don't be afraid to incorporate places or opportunities for more rough-and-tumble activities like dancing, laser tag, or even sports. Don't laugh! While I haven't yet created a half-pipe indoor space, a few years ago I redid a historically important house designed by the early-twentieth-century architect George Washington Smith (sadly, no relation!) and discovered it had a genuine ballroom—a gorgeous and unused space with pink terrazzo floors, tall Spanish-style windows, a fantastic painted ceiling, and even an orchestra balcony. To make this space really versatile, all the linen-slipcovered curved sofas that made up the new seating areas had casters

Your environment can transform how you live and feel, but it's your personal dreams that inform it and give it purpose. When it comes to inspiration, be open-minded and go for what delights you. Whether it's a classic piece or a thrift-store find, let the lines and age of a piece add its voice to that history.

(*following spread*) Every designer has their favorite room—this has to be mine! It has everything I love: gorgeous symmetry, beautiful boiserie, provocative art, diverse chairs in similar fabrics, antiques and contemporary photography. The herringbone parquet was reclaimed from a seventeenth-century château in Lyons; its unexpected and imperfect surface adds an edgy element of rough luxe—one would be as perfectly at home here in a faded pair of jeans or a satin couture gown. It is more than a lovely space, it provides the foundation for the lifestyle of someone who is present in the world in a very deliberate way (gray Westphalian gelding not included).

so that they could be rolled to the corners for gatherings and dancing parties (that orchestra balcony really did come in handy!). The added benefit to having such "adjustable" furnishings is that that the family uses that former white elephant of a room to play roller hockey on weekend afternoons; it's their favorite place to hang out. A house needs those juxtapositions of elegance versus ease, calm as opposed to boisterous, high versus low—one heightens the effect of the other.

Balance is also about the more intangible aspects of life. While we crave a feeling of connectedness to things that are familiar, comfortable, and traditional, far too often we ignore or sideline things that should be playing a more active role in our lives. Many of us have closets stuffed with possessions that we acquired because we just "had to have" them at the time—and then put away and never used. Rather than build walk-in closets that take up unnecessary square footage and encourage people to accumulate more stuff, I prefer to design beautiful built-in cabinetry throughout the home. If kitchens are designed with beautiful cabinets so that wedding china, crystal, and silverware are visible and accessible, they get more use than if they are stored away in "out of sight, out of mind" felt bags in a cupboard. If we luxuriate in using these "special occasion" possessions for a shared dinner, or for that first morning cup of coffee or tea, it serves as a reminder of the day we got married—and, more importantly, *why* we got married. To my mind, there's no such thing as "too good" for every day—we should use the things we love and cherish, and consider divesting ourselves of those that we don't.

My goal is not only to create rooms in which a balance of comfort and elegance can coexist naturally, but to create a setting that people can live in as they write new chapters in their lives. This perspective shapes our new design paradigms for style, taste, practicality, and the art of living in a multidimensional world.

My love affair with silver began when I was given a tiny sterling locket as a child. I've applied this precious-metal finish to drapery rods, curtain rings, fireplace grates and tools, and even three little cast-iron ants I found at an antiques store in Maine. In metallic form its signature sophistication and ever-varying patinas soothe both the eyes and the soul; in softly iridescent fabrics it brings a unique and fascinating luster to any space.

This salon-like retreat is in the center of the house, where every living room ought to be— we might really live in them if they were.

The landscape outside the French doors inspired the theme for this room. The shimmery water-like tones in the opalescent wall coverings and matte metallic fabrics, mother-of-pearl-inlaid Moroccan pieces, and mercury glass in the secretary play against the deep-water blues in the billowing couture taffeta at the French doors and intense indigo base notes in the couch. The chandelier resembles curved fern leaves fashioned from hundreds of luminous crystal icicles— it's unusual, fun, and drop-dead elegant.

(*above and opposite*) Where would we be without hand-painted de Gournay chinoiserie wallpapers? These fantastic silk or paper panels take their cue from eighteenth- and nineteenth-century French designs, but, like this ethereal version, are created with contemporary colors and finishes that give them a wonderful modern feel. Birds and gardens are two common themes: my favorites are finches, partridges, and turtledoves. They are associated with love, happiness, and courtship, so I like to include them in sculptures and other design choices.

Hans Nadelhoffer

Cartier

VAN GOGH

Bathrooms should feel
like actual rooms, rather
than just places to shower
or shave. They should
inspire romance, intimacy,
a feeling of relaxation.

(*previous spread*) Symmetry creates balance and cohesion and brings a timeless order to an architectural space, as does the pairing of classical and contemporary pieces. But deliberately breaking the rules is sometimes the best way to enhance the story and add real personality to a room. This casual jute rug is an unexpected component in a formal space—it's like decorating Prozac because it really unbuttons this lavish salon.

The master bathroom is one of the most important spaces in the house and should be large, spacious—and meant for two. Nothing promotes intimacy like cleaning your teeth next to your loved one, and a larger, shared space encourages you to relax and get reacquainted. It's the ultimate retreat, where you go to unwind, escape, and get away from it all. The accessibility of the garden right outside the doors encourages that letting down of barriers; there's nothing like starting the day by taking a quiet moment, cup of tea in hand, to experience the morning literally coming across the threshold and into the room to greet you.

(*previous spread*) Rather than waste this gorgeous real estate on a walk-in closet that would encourage accumulation for its own sake, it's devoted to a luxurious full-size dressing and sitting room. Rejecting the concept of separate "his" and "hers" areas, the shared space transforms the master suite into a true sanctuary. This intimate spa-like lounge features a freestanding bath that encourages a long, indulgent soak and a stylish and comfortable chaise-type sofa that's perfect for reading or recharging your batteries with a restorative afternoon catnap. Beautiful built-in paneled cabinetry with custom hardware not only reduces clutter but holds far more clothing and accessories than you'd think possible.

Symmetry isn't the only thing that creates balance in this connecting bathroom. As any kindergarten-age child will tell you, sharing is the most important thing. (Flushing comes second!) My own boys shared a bedroom and bath, and it helped them maintain a balance in their relationship that they never outgrew. Separate medicine cabinets and sinks prevent toothpaste wars, twin campaign-style leather-wrapped porthole mirrors allow peacocking without traffic jams, and individual hampers cater to the sensibilities of the cootie-conscious, so the occupants should easily be able to work out the rest of the petty details.

The art on your walls can be as revealing as reading the pages of your diary. It should never be an arbitrary choice just to fill an empty wall or—even worse—to match the sofa.

}

Whether it's sculpture, a canvas, or your child's handprint in clay, the appeal of artwork is incredibly subjective. But no matter the form it takes, it should be selected not because someone told you it was a great investment, or was signifi-cant in some other way, but because of what it means to you. It should be a way to express something vital about yourself to others—to share your sense of fun or worldview through something that speaks to you on an extremely personal level.

There is no better inspiration for design than travel and exposure to other cultures and environments; the eye-opening experiences that result are all grist for the mill.

(*previous spread*) It's the height of irony that only through the modern technology that allows the glass house to exist can we be so in touch with nature. Turning a glass house into a home, while still respecting the lines and angles of the architecture, can be challenging. The neutral palette provides a tabula rasa gallery setting—the highly approachable artwork has a strong organic quality that brings a basic primodial note to the clean modern structure. Post-modernist furniture takes its color cue from the surrounding earth and sky, and keeps to a low profile so as not to challenge the view—or the treasures that surround it.

Your memories (and acquisitions!) from one trip will color your design choices for years to come. On a recent trip to Barcelona, Frank Gehry's steel goldfish sculpture made a huge impact—there's architectural eye candy around every corner of that art-conscious city, but the skeletal and geometric quality of this work, and the way all of its straight lines function together to create a moving form, exerts a special fascination. These abstract mesh and wood sculptures from South America capture that same sinuous, wiry strength.

In a well-edited room, a minimum of elements tell the story. What you leave out is as important as what you put in.

The soaring windows of this glass pavilion flood the open-plan interior with clear, pure California coastal light that highlights every grain and pattern. The heady mix of rough-hewn and far-flung tribal forms and textures creates a charged, globally ethnic current that plays off the smooth polished-stone flooring and crisp, pure geometry of the supporting space. The stylized spindle-back chairs and open basket weave of the table highlight that organic sensibility.

A home in balance is masculine and feminine, antique and modern, light and dark, austere and glam, rustic and sophisticated—all these things in perfect harmony.

The garden room at the end of this house was never used, and my clients wanted to turn it into the husband's writing studio. The south-facing room received wonderful light at the end of the day, and I could see it as being the perfect spot for cocktails at dusk. I had an image of guests mingling in the space, strolling in and out of the adjacent gardens through the open French doors, so I pulled that idea inside by covering the walls in a metallic-silver silk paper and had an artist hand-paint it with trees and flowers in gouache. When the couple hosted their first party in the finished space, the evening light reflected off the silver walls and turned them a warm, glowing copper. The effect was magical—almost as remarkable as the transformation of a once-neglected room into a beloved and well-used space.

(*following spread, left and right*) A handsome Empire desk gives the space a quality of timeless sophistication as it claims the middle ground; a custom-patterned silk rug and elegant *blanc de chine* porcelain glam up the rest of the room. A centuries-old European fascination with all things Asian led to a tradition of placing chic chinoiserie fantasies and actual pieces, like this nineteenth-century lacquered screen and cabinet, alongside Western furnishings. Their exotic grace goes hand in hand with a sense of old-fashioned expert craftsmanship.

I try to combine elements of the formal and the casual in new ways that feel right for today. Contemporary decorating is all about finding that balance.

A Regency-style sofa upholstered in rich silk-velvet adds another provocative twist on texture to this eclectic living room. Applying white lacquer to a classic shape brings a fresh, contemporary look to the piece, and gives timeless elegance a head-turning twist—it's amazing how a color that's "now" can bring about an unexpected and dramatic change.

(*following spread*) An unconventionally artistic household expresses itself in this subtle tone-on-tone balance study. The scale of the former great room was so large that any rug that fit looked like it was originally made for a stuffy embassy ballroom, so I stitched together four separate indigo patchwork rugs into one huge carpet. The result was truly bohemian chic: a unique silk tapestry that had a Janis Joplin vagabond vibe all its own. It literally laid the groundwork that allowed both formal and eccentric elements in the new living room to come together.

(*above and opposite*) The collected room is both eclectic and soulful; it speaks of well-earned relaxation amid the spoils from years of world travel. The ornately scrolled Venetian mirror from the 1920s evokes a special sort of nostalgia—it would have enhanced any of Gatsby's fabulous parties. The intriguing, delicate half-tone patterns on the wall fabric are reminiscent of faded watermarks on the walls of a palazzo off the Grand Canal; the mirror's delicious curlicues and worn patina take up that subtle whispered cue, turning it into a definitive statement.

Having a dance background means I approach interior design from a different perspective.

While dance training imparts a unique viewpoint of space, and guidance in terms of what flows and what doesn't, there's still no better career example to follow than Elsie de Wolfe, who also started out in the theater before creating the occupation of interior designer. While there have been many important decorators and influential schools of design since she first swept away the ugly bric-a-brac and clutter that defined the Victorian style a century ago, she was still the first to recognize that comfort and personal lifestyle were actual design innovations.

(following spread) A formerly cluttered bedroom is transformed into a soothing refuge that guarantees a peaceful night's sleep. The clean lines of the architecture and the art are softened by the graceful scroll-arm sofa and the curves of the lushly upholstered luxury-ocean-liner-style berth. The lovely turn-of-the-century ballroom-style crystal fixture and Chippendale-style fretwork in the sumptuous cross-grain *bibliothèque* add a complementary note of history.

ACKNOWLEDGMENTS

The gratitude I have for my clients is beyond my ability to adequately express. It's an enormous privilege for a designer to help create a home, and to be given the opportunity to create rooms where people live their lives, raise their children, and make a lifetime of memories is something that should never be taken lightly. I thank them for the great gift of their trust, confidence and friendship—and then, after the final picture is hung and dinner is in the oven, for their extraordinary generosity in allowing me to share with others a glimpse—or three—into their private homes.

If you're very fortunate, there are special people in your life who defy categorization; to try to define them within the confines of friendship is an exercise in futility as they always exceed that limitation with ridiculous ease. I truly hit that fabled serendipity jackpot when it allowed me to connect with Gwyneth Paltrow. She does me an enormous honor by writing the foreword: from one daddy's girl to another, the admiration, love, and respect I hold for her cannot be measured.

In my next life, I want to come back as Michael Bruno. His vision and design sense are truly unique, but what I treasure most about him is his warmth, loyalty and wise counsel. The rapport we share has made him like a brother to me, only without all that fighting over who got the bigger dessert.

I'm truly grateful for the grounded love and support of my siblings Doug and Martha—they know that you really do have to throw a lot of macaroni against the wall to get it to stick—and for my wonderful mother-in-law Dot, who can never visit often or long enough.

I owe so much to my dearest friend and mentor Roger Birnbaum, for his constant enthusiasm and firm belief that I could, indeed, build one helluva house, and to Louise Lanning for believing in the kismet of a misdialed number.

I would be lost without the savvy and intuitive Laurie Salmore, who helps harness my creative dreams and visions and make them a reality. Her strategic guidance is beyond value, and when it comes to rolling her sleeves up and taking on a project there is virtually nothing she says "no" to!

Since Kathryn Ireland nurtured my design career and watched it grow up alongside our respective children, a large part of the blame is hers. Her selfless encouragement and open-handed generosity are beyond price. She, along with my other colleague, Martyn Lawrence Bullard, were an invaluable resource, and not just because they are delightful dining and shopping companions who can take last-minute disasters as well as an erupting Icelandic volcano in their stride.

My favorite place on earth is amidst the cheering section of my lifelong friends Karen Pulaski, Marty and Aleeza Callner, and Cindy Gold, and not just because they are the source of all my sound bites and don't make me pay royalties.

I never would have even considered embarking on this book without the active encouragement of my many friends and supporters in the editorial community, among them Ann Maine,

Carolyn Englefield, Clint Smith, Dara Caponigro, Deborah Needleman, Jay Fielden, Jennifer Levine Bruno, Jennifer Smith Hale, Margaret Russell, Michael Boodro, Newell Turner, Orli Ben-Dor, Pam Jaccarino and Steven Drucker. After the past year, my real understanding and appreciation for what they do on a daily basis to get a story published has grown by leaps and bounds.

My deepest appreciation for seeing the potential in this book and then turning it into a reality goes to my agent Jill Cohen, who encouraged me from the start and never let me give up; to Kathleen Jayes, my steadfast editor; and to Charles Miers, publisher of Rizzoli International Publications: their unflagging guidance, encouragement, and genuine appreciation of my work has been a sustaining force throughout this project. My profound gratitude goes to Doug Turshen and Steve Turner for their tenacity and patience in transforming an overwhelming amount of images into an eloquent photo essay.

I am in awe of the incredibly talented photographers represented here: for their imagination, patience, and critical eye, for their determination to stretch the magic hour to a full ninety minutes, and for refusing to quit before they capture that one elusive moment that makes a space resonate.

A special thank you to Meredith Strang for the eleventh hour rescue with an arsenal of great historical references, so that they weren't all squandered on bar trivia contests and "Jeopardy". She not only captured my aesthetic, but her words helped to give my passion for design a voice in print.

My heartfelt gratitude goes to the engineers, architects, and contractors that have collaborated with me on all these homes, and to all the amazing artisans, carpenters, upholsterers, restorers, and artists whose workrooms have produced such unique and amazing objects; their remarkable translation of my visions into physical form have helped make these rooms possible. I am equally indebted to Kravet, Century Furniture, Arteriors, and Boyd Lighting; the numerous opportunities they gave me to develop a design presence represents the type of collaboration that is mostly undreamt of.

An earnest thank you goes to the incredibly creative and dedicated Sarah Hall and Alexandra Hall of Harley & Co. for their outstanding performance in coordinating promotion and marketing, and to my partners Julia Sorkin and Elisabeth Weinstock, for believing that a crazy design notion conceived at my kitchen table could grow up to become Room in a Box.

I would be remiss if I didn't thank my legal eagles Brian Weinhart and Anthony Keats, Esquires, for always making sure all our i's are crossed and our t's are dotted.

And last, but certainly never least, my loving appreciation and sincerest thanks to my tireless office team; there's no one like them for keeping things on track, on time, and in focus. To have maintained that performance throughout the months of extra work involved in creating this book without either missing a beat or losing their minds is a real testament to their devotion, dedication to excellence, and the powers of Excedrin.

PHOTOGRAPHY CREDITS

Melanie Acevedo: endpapers; pp. 4; 44-45; 46-47; 48-49; 50-51; 87; 88-89; 90; 91; 94-95; 97; 98-99; 103; 104; 105; 107; 108-109; 110; 111; 113; 114-115; 118-119; 136-137; 138-139; 144-145; 154-155; 158-159; 168-169; 172-173; 175; 176-177; 187; 188-189; 199; 200-201; 202; 203; 204-205; 208; 245; 246-247; 248; 249; 252-253.

Michael Wells: pp. 2-3; 9; 28; 35; 36-37; 43 (lower left, lower right); 73; 74-75; 77; 78-79; 116; 117; 120-121; 122-123; 135; 148-149; 150-151; 180-181; 183; 184-185; 209; 213; 219; 220-221; 222; 223; 224-225; 251

Victoria Pearson: pp. 15; 16-17; 82-83; 93; 124-125; 128-129; 130; 133; 157; 161; 207; 234-235; 233; 237; 238-239

Luca Trovato: pp. 18; 20-21; 29; 30-31; 32-33; 39; 40-41; 43 (upper left); 53; 54; 55; 81; 192; 195; 196; 215; 216-217; 227; 228-229; 230-231

Max Kim-Bee: pp. 22-23; 25; 26-27; 191; 193

Tim Street-Porter: pp. 56; 57; 58; 59; 60-61; 62; 63

Justin Coit Photography/Artmix Creative: pp. 67; 68-69; 70

Dennis Gibbens, Architect: pp. 141; 142-143

Pablo Enriquez: pp. 162; 164-165

Peter Vitale: p. 160

Edmund Barr, courtesy *Traditional Home*: p. 153

Lisa Romerein: pp. 43 (upper right); 84-85; 100-101; 166-167; 179; 197; 241; 242; 243

Cindy Gold Photography: p. 147

First published in the United States of America in 2015
by Rizzoli International Publications, Inc.
300 Park Avenue South
New York, NY 10010
www.rizzoliusa.com

2015 2016 2017 2018 / 10 9 8 7 6 5 4 3 2 1

Distributed in the U.S. trade by Random House, New York

Designed by Doug Turshen with Steve Turner

Printed in China

ISBN-13: 978-0-8478-4362-6

Library of Congress Catalog Control Number: 2014956042

Justine Picardie CHANEL – HER LIFE Streidl

CASA ALTA

Through the LABYRINTH

REFLECTION OF A MAN

Hortus Eystettensis The Bishop's Garden and Besler's Magnificent Book

18